Traffic Lig

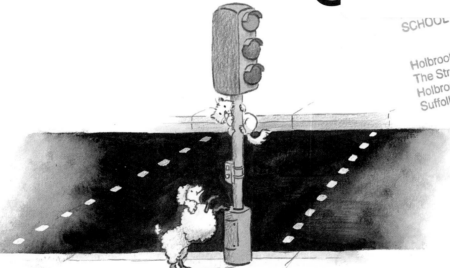

Written by Maire Buonocore
Illustrated by Natalie Bould

Collins Educational
An imprint of HarperCollinsPublishers

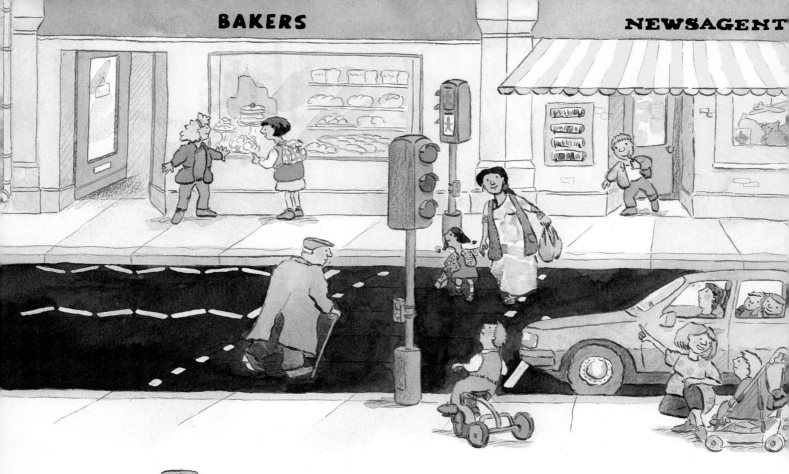

A red light.

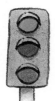

2

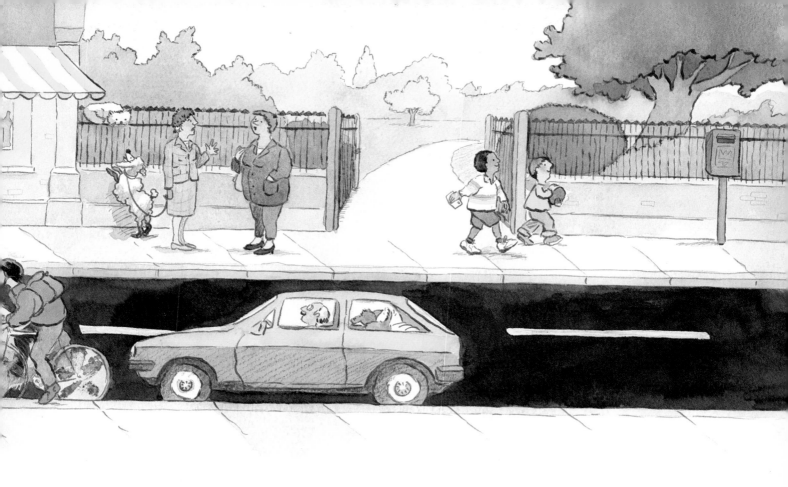

We wait.

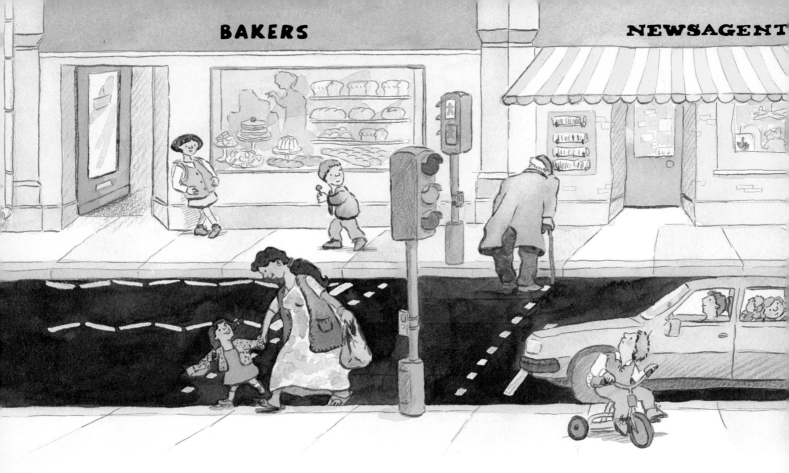

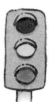 An amber light flashes.

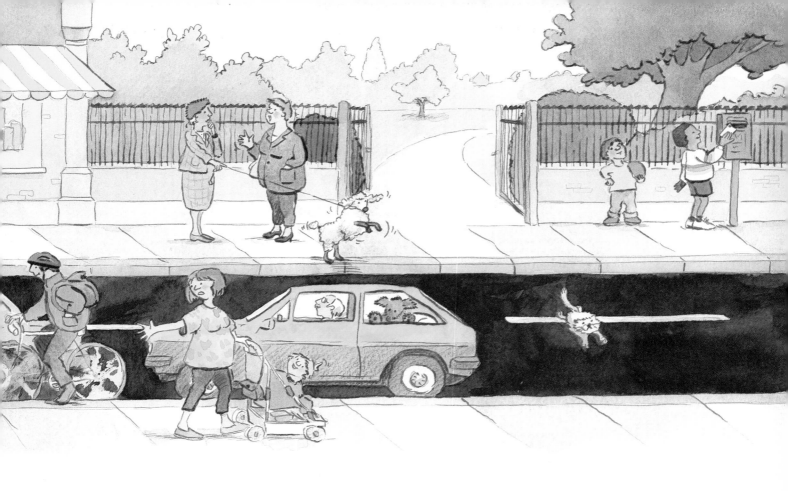

We wait.

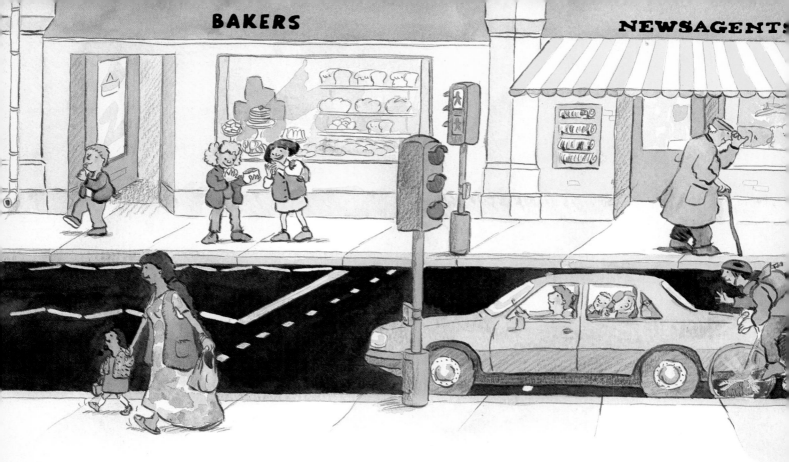

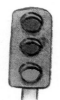

A green light.

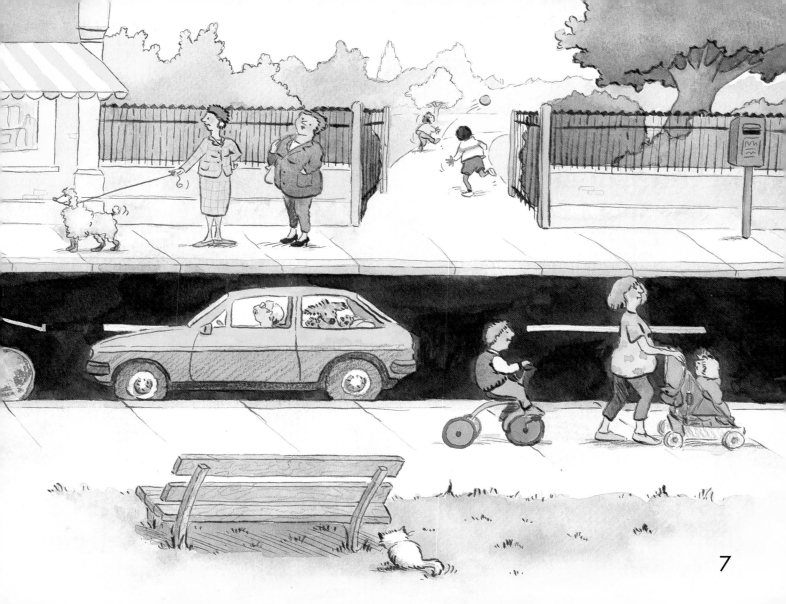

7

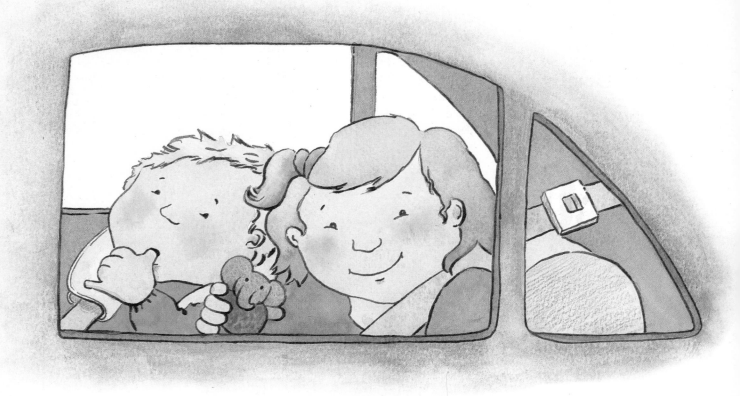

Off we go.